Reducing Tensions Between Russia and NATO

COUNCIL *on*
FOREIGN
RELATIONS

Center for Preventive Action

Council Special Report No. 79
March 2017

Kimberly Marten

Reducing Tensions Between Russia and NATO

The Council on Foreign Relations (CFR) is an independent, nonpartisan membership organization, think tank, and publisher dedicated to being a resource for its members, government officials, business executives, journalists, educators and students, civic and religious leaders, and other interested citizens in order to help them better understand the world and the foreign policy choices facing the United States and other countries. Founded in 1921, CFR carries out its mission by maintaining a diverse membership, with special programs to promote interest and develop expertise in the next generation of foreign policy leaders; convening meetings at its headquarters in New York and in Washington, DC, and other cities where senior government officials, members of Congress, global leaders, and prominent thinkers come together with Council members to discuss and debate major international issues; supporting a Studies Program that fosters independent research, enabling CFR scholars to produce articles, reports, and books and hold roundtables that analyze foreign policy issues and make concrete policy recommendations; publishing *Foreign Affairs*, the preeminent journal on international affairs and U.S. foreign policy; sponsoring Independent Task Forces that produce reports with both findings and policy prescriptions on the most important foreign policy topics; and providing up-to-date information and analysis about world events and American foreign policy on its website, CFR.org.

The Council on Foreign Relations takes no institutional positions on policy issues and has no affiliation with the U.S. government. All views expressed in its publications and on its website are the sole responsibility of the author or authors.

Council Special Reports (CSRs) are concise policy briefs, produced to provide a rapid response to a developing crisis or contribute to the public's understanding of current policy dilemmas. CSRs are written by individual authors—who may be CFR fellows or acknowledged experts from outside the institution—in consultation with an advisory committee, and are intended to take sixty days from inception to publication. The committee serves as a sounding board and provides feedback on a draft report. It usually meets twice—once before a draft is written and once again when there is a draft for review; however, advisory committee members, unlike Task Force members, are not asked to sign off on the report or to otherwise endorse it. Once published, CSRs are posted on www.cfr.org.

For further information about CFR or this Special Report, please write to the Council on Foreign Relations, 58 East 68th Street, New York, NY 10065, or call the Communications office at 212.434.9888. Visit our website, CFR.org.

To submit a letter in response to a Council Special Report for publication on our website, CFR.org, you may send an email to CSReditor@cfr.org. Alternatively, letters may be mailed to us at: Publications Department, Council on Foreign Relations, 58 East 68th Street, New York, NY 10065. Letters should include the writer's name, postal address, and daytime phone number. Letters may be edited for length and clarity, and may be published online. Please do not send attachments. All letters become the property of the Council on Foreign Relations and will not be returned. We regret that, owing to the volume of correspondence, we cannot respond to every letter.

This report is printed on paper that is FSC ® Chain-of-Custody Certified by a printer who is certified by BM TRADA North America Inc.

Contents

Foreword

Since the end of the Cold War and the dissolution of the Soviet Union, the relationship between the United States and Russia often has been difficult and, in recent years, worse than that. From the American perspective, the fault lies clearly with Russia, the result of Russia's 2014 invasion and annexation of Crimea, its continued incursions in eastern Ukraine ever since, its intervention in Syria on behalf of a brutal regime, and its use of hacking and cyberattacks to tamper with the 2016 U.S. presidential election. From Russia's vantage point, the blame falls squarely on the United States, and stems from enlargement of the North Atlantic Treaty Organization (NATO), American-led military interventions in Europe and the Middle East, a perceived lack of respect for Russia, and the belief that Washington seeks regime change in Moscow. Whatever the perceptions, the reality is that Russia remains a major power willing to use its modern military and seat on the UN Security Council to pursue its interests. As a result, what has become clear is that the United States needs to act deliberately if it hopes to temper Russia's actions beyond its borders and perhaps create a more constructive relationship between the two countries.

In this new Council Special Report, Kimberly Marten, a professor of political science at Barnard College, at Columbia University, and director of the program on U.S.-Russia relations at Columbia's Harriman Institute, addresses the rising tensions between Russia and both the United States and the rest of NATO. Marten is convincing when she writes about the tensions between NATO and Russia—tensions that could boil over into conflict if there were an accidental or intentional encounter between Russian and NATO militaries, a Russian incursion into NATO territory, or a hybrid war that included cyberattacks and sowing seeds of discontent in Eastern Europe.

Marten also recommends several policy steps that the United States and NATO should take to avoid any such crisis. She weighs the needs of deterrence—including the United States publicly committing to uphold NATO's defense clause, positioning troops in vulnerable NATO countries, and enhancing cyber defense and offense capabilities across the NATO bloc—and reassurance—including treating Russian President Vladimir Putin and other Russian leaders with respect, refraining from undermining each other's domestic political stability (including formally stating that the United States does not seek Russian regime change), reestablishing arms control negotiations and agreements, and halting further NATO expansion, especially in Ukraine. Operating firmly in the tradition of foreign policy realism, Marten makes the case that both deterrence and reassurance measures are necessary and can in fact work in harmony.

The stakes are indeed high. So far this century, major powers have avoided conflict, but the current era is rife with other regional issues, including an unraveling Middle East, economic stagnation and political discontent across Europe, and tension in Asia over a rising China and reckless North Korea. Not only would a crisis between Russia and NATO compound this daunting foreign policy landscape, but it would result in a missed opportunity for both sides to work together on tackling some of the world's greatest challenges. The new U.S. administration would be wise to consider Marten's advice as it develops a policy toward Russia that manages to avoid being passive on one hand and overly confrontational on the other.

Richard N. Haass
President
Council on Foreign Relations
March 2017

Acknowledgments

My deepest gratitude goes to CFR President Richard N. Haass, Senior Vice President and Director of Studies James M. Lindsay, Director of the Center for Preventive Action Paul B. Stares, and Micah Zenko for giving me the opportunity to write this report and for useful comments and criticism along the way; to Jennifer Wilson and Sarah Collman for their able administrative assistance; and to Micah and Jennifer especially for their continuing encouragement and heroic efforts to condense one of my earlier drafts. I am grateful beyond words to members of the advisory committee who shared their supportive criticisms and suggestions for improvements with me, especially Committee Chair Angela Stent and William Courtney, Heidi Crebo-Rediker, Karen Lea Dawisha, James M. Goldgeier, Thomas Edward Graham, David J. Kramer, Robert Legvold, Jeffrey Mankoff, Cynthia Roberts, Stephen R. Sestanovich, David R. Slade, Julianne C. Smith, and Constanze Stelzenmüller, as well as Paul B. Stares and Micah Zenko once again.

I am also extraordinarily grateful to all of the additional policymakers and analysts who agreed to speak with me as I wrote this report. Some wish to remain on background, but my thanks go publicly to Daniel Fried, Austin Long, Wolfgang Richter, Brad Roberts, Strobe Talbott, and Alexander Vershbow. I also want to thank Robert J. Elder for a conversation several years ago that first sparked these ideas and Niall Henderson for able research assistance on Russian force levels. These individuals do not necessarily agree with my arguments, nor did I take all of the advice that was given. The statements made in this report are solely my own. This publication was made possible by a grant from Carnegie Corporation of New York.

Kimberly Marten

Acronyms

ABM	Anti-Ballistic Missile
A/CFE	"adapted" CFE
A2/AD	anti-access/area denial
BMD	ballistic missile defense
CFE	Conventional Forces in Europe
C4I	command, control, communication, computer, and intelligence
DNC	Democratic National Committee
EU	European Union
GDP	gross domestic product
INF	Intermediate-Range Nuclear Forces
NATO	North Atlantic Treaty Organization
NRFA	NATO-Russia Founding Act
SWIFT	Society for Worldwide Interbank Financial Telecommunication

Map by the Council on Foreign Relations.

Council Special Report

Introduction

As Donald J. Trump begins his presidency, U.S. leaders—including senior members of the Senate, military commanders and intelligence officials, and some of Trump's own cabinet picks—are extraordinarily divided about how to define U.S. security interests toward Russia. As a candidate, Trump shocked observers by calling into question the wisdom of the U.S. commitment to defend its North Atlantic Treaty Organization (NATO) allies from Russian aggression, at a time when NATO's Supreme Commander, U.S. Air Force General Philip Breedlove, had labeled Russia an "existential threat." The U.S. presidential election and its aftermath were plagued with controversies about how to interpret and respond to Russia's state-sponsored hacking of the emails of the Democratic National Committee (DNC) and major Democratic Party figures, while some U.S. allies in Europe feared their own electoral processes would be the next victims. Trump's efforts to reach out to Russian President Vladimir Putin and launch another "reset" policy may lead to new accord between the two countries, but some experts fear that Putin will test Trump's strength by seeking unequal advantages for Moscow. In December 2016, Putin and Trump publicly flirted with the idea of a new nuclear arms race, even as they pledged cooperation.

Resolving these debates requires in-depth analysis of how the United States can best secure its own interests amid great tension between NATO and Russia in the European military theater. With careful, concrete policy measures, Washington can avoid an unthinking slide down either of two dangerous paths in this time of uncertainty and change. On the one hand, the United States should resist the calls from politicians and policy experts to strongly increase its NATO conventional force presence. To do so could spark an expensive arms race with Russia that would heighten instability in Europe and could even provoke Moscow to use military force against one or more NATO countries. It could also tempt Moscow to lessen its cooperation with Washington on other important global issues, such as preventing nuclear proliferation by rogue states, battling international terrorism, and continuing crucial scientific cooperation in the Arctic and outer space. Furthermore, it is unnecessary, since more creative approaches can deter Russian aggression without a dangerous, expensive military buildup in Europe. On the other hand, the United States should avoid squandering its global reputation for strength and reliability by allowing its oldest and most venerable alliance to collapse in the face of Russian threats. Putin has taken a series of actions designed to intimidate the West and demonstrate his willingness and ability to fight, and it would be foolish for the Trump administration to ignore the real challenges Russia presents to U.S. and European security.

Since occupying the Ukrainian province of Crimea in March 2014, Putin and his supporters have encouraged unrest in the Donbas region of eastern Ukraine and sent thousands of Russian troops to support rebels there; built up Russia's military forces on its western borders and its naval presence in the Black Sea; publicly threatened NATO members Romania and Poland with nuclear strikes for accepting U.S. missile defense installations; provoked dozens of dangerous military encounters with NATO and other non-NATO Western ships and aircraft; aggravated the refugee crisis in Europe by carpet-bombing areas of Syria; deployed air defense forces in Syria capable of targeting NATO flights in eastern Turkey and along Turkey's Mediterranean coastline; and waged an information war against the West, including cyber espionage and interference in Western political processes. Putin's aggression makes the possibility of a war in Europe between nuclear-armed adversaries frighteningly real. The fact that both sides have allowed their arms control regimes to atrophy adds further danger to the relationship.

Yet the ultimate intentions of Putin and his regime, as well as those of his eventual successors, are unknowable. Russia may seek to break the NATO alliance or even expand at NATO's expense—to reconquer lost Soviet territory, to attain regional hegemony in Eurasia, or to allow Putin to go down in history as the man who reestablished Russia's great power status. But Russian aggression may also reflect fear—or even paranoia—about Western intentions to use regime change to create a democratic "whole and free" Europe. Putin is fixated on the notion that the United States wants to overthrow his regime. Russian military officers, politicians, and large swaths of the Russian public seem genuinely to believe that NATO is encircling Russia and threatening the Russian homeland. NATO's enlargement to include a dozen new European members after Germany's 1990 reunification has been a major irritant. Even more disturbing to Moscow has been the willingness of the United States and its Western allies to wage air strikes and wars beyond NATO borders, with or without UN Security Council approval and in the face of Russia's Security Council veto.

Amidst these uncertainties, NATO cohesion has frayed. Central and East European allies, including Poland and the Baltic states of Estonia, Latvia, and Lithuania, fear that growing U.S. isolationism will leave them undefended against Russian aggression. If the Russian military were to establish a beachhead in the Baltic region beyond the Kaliningrad exclave, or elsewhere to its west, Germany would also be threatened. Yet many NATO members have faced significant losses in trade because of Western sanctions against Russia. Several U.S. allies, including France, Hungary, and the United Kingdom, have growing far-right nationalist political parties that denigrate NATO and welcome cooperation with Putin.[1] There is evidence that some extremist movements in Europe are supported by Moscow.[2] NATO's internal tensions were exacerbated by the failed July 2016 coup attempt in Turkey and subsequent crackdown against the Turkish armed forces by President Recep Tayyip Erdogan. Many Turks blamed the U.S. military for the coup, and Erdogan reached out to Putin in the aftermath, signing a ceasefire accord in Syria without U.S. participation and coordinating airstrikes with Russia in northern Syria.

To avoid military crises between Russia and NATO in the face of uncertainty about Russia's intentions, the United States should work with its NATO allies to simultaneously deter a potentially aggressive Russia while reassuring a potentially frightened Russia. Washington should dissuade Moscow from threatening NATO member states and communicate that U.S. defensive commitments to its allies are firm and reliable, while emphasizing that these commitments are intended neither to isolate Russia from the West nor to initiate regime change in Moscow. The United States will have an easier time demonstrating defensive intent, avoiding Russian charges of hypocrisy, and bringing European allies on board if decisions are based on consistent, transparent, and treaty- and rule-based criteria.

None of these suggested approaches should be read as a concession to Putin. A minimally enhanced and creatively constructed set of deterrent measures can prevent Russian military aggression and keep the United States and its allies safe, without requiring any reciprocation from Russia. Putin can build up Russian military forces all he wants (and perhaps even do significant damage to the Russian economy in the process). But as long as he is dissuaded from attacking NATO territory, NATO wins.

Why NATO Matters

Throughout the Cold War, U.S. leaders and politicians frequently called for more NATO burden-sharing because the United States always assumed an outsize responsibility for NATO financing and troop deployments. Until recently, though, no mainstream U.S. foreign policy analysis would have needed to justify the U.S. commitment to NATO's defense. Commitment was assumed, even amid pitched debates about how much of the defense budget or how many U.S. troops should be designated for that purpose.

That changed in 2016, when then-candidate Trump surprised leaders of the Republican Party and the Pentagon—not to mention U.S. allies—by calling NATO obsolete and arguing that the defense of particular NATO members should be made conditional on their financial contributions to the alliance. Trump seemed to be disavowing Article 5 of the 1949 NATO Charter, which says that an external military attack against one member will be treated as an attack against all. Trump's statements served as a wake-up call about the need to explain why defending the NATO alliance is in the U.S. national interest.

NATO still matters because it is a flexible and reliable institution that provides security to some of the United States' most important allies: stable democracies in Canada and Europe. Having strong, like-minded European partners helps expand the global reach of U.S. values and authority, so protecting European freedom enhances U.S. influence and credibility abroad. The United States also has an enduring economic interest in protecting these countries from foreign threats because Europe is its largest trade and investment partner. U.S. exports to Europe and European investments in the United States contribute to American jobs and the U.S. tax base, and the strength of this economic relationship depends on Europe's well-being.

Because of these cultural and economic ties, any war that threatens the stability of Europe would eventually drag in U.S. military forces, as happened in World War I, World War II, and the Yugoslavian civil wars of the 1990s, despite strong initial calls in each case for a more isolationist approach. Preventing war and enhancing stability in Europe is therefore in U.S. interests, as is maintaining a well-integrated military alliance structure at high readiness to meet any threats that arise.

Although the Soviet Union, NATO's original adversary, is gone, many analysts consider Putin's crackdowns on Russian media and civil society and his recentralization of state control over the Russian economy as the start of a re-Sovietization of Russian life. The strength of NATO, backed by the guarantee of the U.S. extended nuclear deterrent, succeeded for fifty years in containing what might otherwise have been Soviet attempts at territorial expansion. To condemn NATO allies to face a potential new Russian threat on their own would irreparably harm the United States' reputation for reliability and integrity, permanently damaging its ability to exert influence abroad. NATO allies supported the United States in Afghanistan after the 9/11 attacks, when Article 5 was invoked for the only time in NATO history. Estonia and Latvia, two former Soviet Baltic states often mentioned as potential Russian targets today, lost soldiers in Afghanistan and sent troops to help the U.S.-led coalition in Iraq. To abandon those countries now would give the United States a reputation for hypocrisy and ingratitude.

Although some NATO members have failed to live up to the alliance's democratic ideals, their integration into the NATO community and continuing desire for the security benefits it provides may serve as a brake on what otherwise could be untrammeled authoritarianism. At a time of growing ethnic nationalism in Europe, NATO's integration of European military command structures and the continued European reliance on U.S. intelligence and force projection capabilities through NATO is especially important. One of NATO's early purposes was not merely to deter the Soviet threat but to bring postwar German military forces into the alliance structure and calm French fears of a third world war. NATO was a crucial enabler of peace not only after World War II but also after the Cold War because some Europeans feared that German reunification in 1990 could create a new military juggernaut. NATO's military integration now means that even if right-wing nationalists were to rule a European state, they could not threaten their neighbors without a drastic and expensive overhaul of force capabilities, deployments, infrastructure, and policy, providing a long warning time for any possible aggression. NATO continues to provide protection not merely from Russia but within Europe itself.

The Growth of NATO-Russia Tensions

When the Cold War ended, hopes were high for a new partnership between Russia and the West. But the relationship soon soured, repeating a cycle of attempted cooperation followed by disappointment.[3] A deep sense of Russian shame over lost influence in the world was coupled with grievance over Western indifference to Russian interests and what many Russians saw as Western betrayal. This was matched by growing Western disappointment that the Kremlin did not choose to join the Western world order and a belief that Russian leaders were unreliable and (in the case of Putin and his allies) perhaps even criminal.

While Russians today often blame NATO enlargement for these tensions, the change in alliance structures did not start in the West, or on NATO's initiative. Instead, it began in the final days of the Soviet Union, when Poland, Hungary, and Czechoslovakia (the so-called Visegrad states) decided to withdraw from the Soviet-led Warsaw Pact. In the 1990 Charter of Paris, Mikhail Gorbachev, the last Soviet leader, officially recognized those states' right to leave the pact and choose their own security arrangements. The Visegrad states desperately wanted to join NATO, but several years passed before the United States and its allies were willing to entertain that possibility. Then in December 1991, on the initiative of its Russian, Ukrainian, and Belarusian republics, the Soviet Union dissolved into fifteen independent countries, several years before NATO considered any new expansion.

As the 1990s wore on, Washington and its allies hoped that NATO enlargement—alongside enlargement of the European Union (EU)—would secure democratic, human rights, and security reforms achieved in East and Central Europe, rewarding new members for their progress along a path that Moscow could have chosen to take, but did not. Russia was instead unstable—with violent upheaval in Moscow's streets during the constitutional crisis of October 1993 and two brutal civil wars in Chechnya—at a time when the West feared ethnic conflict and state failure above all else. NATO's biggest worry at that time was not an expansionist Russia but Russian anarchy and collapse. The Kremlin never established democratic control over its military or intelligence services, leaving the Russian state untrustworthy in Western eyes. President Boris Yeltsin became more authoritarian with time, modifying the Russian constitution to enhance his power, a trend that Putin continued.

NATO was willing to add new members only if they could contribute to the security of the alliance, and most U.S. and Western political leaders feared that offering Russia membership would instead undercut the alliance. U.S. officials nonetheless believed that they worked hard during the 1990s to create a prominent place for Russia in the new security architecture of post–Cold War Europe, pursuing what they called a "two-track policy" of cooperation with Russia alongside NATO enlargement.[4] The West participated in constant high-level negotiations with its Russian counterparts on arms control and other issues. Russia was included in NATO's new Partnership for Peace institutions, designed to enhance cooperation among military forces across the former Cold War divide through joint training and planning, as well as to share best practices for democratic oversight of military organizations. Partnership for Peace was devised in part to ease Russian fears about NATO's intentions by creating new channels for communication among military officers and defense officials and providing a window into NATO operations. Russian forces served side by side with their U.S. and NATO counterparts in peace enforcement operations in Bosnia and Kosovo as part of these Partnership for Peace arrangements.

Despite disagreements about whether the West made implicit promises to Russia about not enlarging NATO, in 1997 both sides signed the NATO-Russia Founding Act (NRFA). The goal of the NRFA was to encourage Russian acceptance of NATO's enlargement by highlighting Russia's importance in European security, giving Moscow a voice and special consultative standing with NATO, but no veto over NATO enlargement or actions.[5] Although Russia was never happy about NATO enlargement, the primary concerns expressed in the 1990s, and even in the early years of Putin's presidency, were not that NATO posed a military threat to Russia. Instead, the fear was that Russia would be cut out of crucial security decisions and be isolated from the West, and that this would aid the rise of extreme nationalists inside Russia.

One issue propelling Russian nationalist sentiment was the notion that Gorbachev had made unilateral concessions to the West: the Warsaw Pact alliance in Eastern Europe disintegrated without incident, Germany reunified peacefully with Soviet help, and individual Soviet republics became newly independent states. In contrast, NATO became more assertive. It used military force for the first time in 1994 when it enforced a no-fly zone in Bosnia during the Yugoslavian civil wars in an "out-of-area" operation that had Russia's approval in the UN Security Council but was not clearly connected to NATO's self-defense mandate. In the ensuing months, NATO carried out airstrikes against Serbian paramilitaries in Bosnia, and Russian support became increasingly grudging. Distrust grew in 1999, when NATO intervened in the Kosovo crisis without Security Council approval and against Russian wishes, again for humanitarian reasons and again against Serbia (by this time considered one of Moscow's allies). NATO believed it was acting ethically to protect threatened Kosovar civilians, and Russia eventually participated in the postwar peace enforcement operation in Kosovo, as it had earlier in Bosnia. But this time NATO showed that it no longer respected one of the only global power tools left for a diminished Russia: its Security Council veto. The U.S.-led invasion of Iraq in 2003 without Security Council approval magnified Russia's sense of irrelevance and frustration. In 2011, Russia was dismayed anew when Security Council–authorized NATO air strikes to protect civilians in Libya morphed against Russian wishes into an effort to support rebels who then toppled and killed leader Muammar al-Qaddafi.

Meanwhile, NATO seemed, in Russian eyes, to welcome almost every state except Russia as a new member: the former Warsaw Pact states, starting with Poland, Hungary, and the Czech Republic, and continuing with Slovakia and the Black Sea states of Romania and Bulgaria; several additional countries in the Balkans, historically viewed as a Russian protectorate; and the three Baltic states of Lithuania, Latvia, and Estonia (former Soviet republics never recognized as such by the West). It was clear to at least some prominent Russian analysts that as soon as NATO began enlarging, the Baltic states, eager to resume their European identity and throw off the Soviet yoke, would also be welcomed in.[6] Putin himself said in 2002 that their membership would be "no tragedy," as long as no new military infrastructure was placed there.[7] But their membership expanded NATO's presence on Russia's borders and left the heavily militarized Russian province of Kaliningrad surrounded by NATO territory.

Government-funded Western organizations also provided advisory and financial assistance to local civil society groups leading revolutionary political efforts, which displaced leaders who had been friendlier to Moscow, in two other post-Soviet states: the 2003 Rose Revolution in Georgia and the 2004 Orange Revolution in Ukraine.[8] Although neither Georgia nor Ukraine has yet been offered a NATO Membership Action Plan—the first step toward joining the alliance—NATO declared in 2008 that both countries "will become members."[9] Later that year, a brief war between Georgia and Russia left Russian forces occupying the contested Georgian territories of South Ossetia and Abkhazia. Then in 2014, during the Euromaidan protests in Kiev, secret recordings publicized by the Kremlin revealed U.S. officials discussing which Ukrainian politicians to support as replacements for the discredited former leader whom Putin favored, Viktor Yanukovych.[10] The 2014 Ukraine crisis came to symbolize everything the Putin regime feared about the West, including the encroachment of the European economic and political model into the traditional Russian sphere of influence, Western support for anti-Putin regime change, and the potential loss of Russian military assets in the Crimean port of Sevastopol. These fears undoubtedly contributed to Putin's decisions to seize Crimea and disrupt the Donbas.

It is unlikely that either Georgia or Ukraine will be invited to join NATO anytime soon, since both states have continuing political, economic, and security weaknesses that would make them liabilities to NATO rather than assets. But Russian troops remain in the internationally recognized territories of both states, at least in part to prevent them from achieving the kind of security and stability that is required for NATO accession.

Understanding Russia

This trajectory helps explain why Putin's bashing of the United States and NATO has received enthusiastic support from the Russian population. The Russian military genuinely fears a surprise Western attack along the country's long borders, including possible U.S. or NATO intervention in one of Russia's ongoing military conflicts.[11] Russia's geography, extending over a large area without natural protection from neighboring powers, has always left it vulnerable—and its history includes numerous attacks from the West, by Charles XII of Sweden in 1708, Napoleon in 1812, and Hitler in 1941 (after large swaths of Russian territory were occupied by German and Austrian troops during World War I). The Russian military was particularly humiliated by its diminished role under Gorbachev and Yeltsin and by critical domestic media coverage in the 1990s and early 2000s, and Putin's new assertiveness against the West has had an appreciative audience inside that institution.

Putin further shores up his domestic standing by blaming all of Russia's ills on nefarious Western interference. The more the United States and NATO remilitarize their relationship with Russia, the more strength Putin and his political allies gain at home. An arms race, despite its budgetary costs, would directly benefit Putin's close friends from the Russian intelligence services, who control the contracting processes in major Russian defense industries and line their pockets with each new weapons purchase.[12] In addition, the Kremlin justifies its crackdown on Russian media freedom and political dissent with accusations of foreign influence and treason, portraying Russia's domestic opposition as part of a Western conspiracy to overthrow the regime.

Putin's hold on power appears stable, and neither popular revolt nor the rise of pro-Western liberals in the Kremlin is likely anytime soon, no matter what happens in U.S.-Russian relations. But the regime is opaque, and growing evidence of disputes within Putin's inner circle, as well as the apparent lack of a designated successor in the event of Putin's death or incapacitation, adds uncertainty. Policymaking in Russia is based on personal connections and informal networks, not bureaucratic hierarchies or formal governmental institutions.[13] No one outside the Kremlin, even within the broader Russian elite, knows for sure how decisions are actually made inside its walls. Tensions within the Russian elite over continuing economic decline could cause Moscow to lash out unpredictably, especially given the rise of ethnic nationalist sentiment in recent years. But Moscow could instead try to lower tensions with the West, perhaps for economic reasons or to cooperate in managing the rise of China. Finding the right balance in security relations with Russia going forward is therefore crucial.

Arms Control Issues

Growing friction between Russia and the West was exacerbated by both sides' willingness to allow the collapse of the arms control framework that had moderated Cold War tensions since the early 1970s. In addition to their literal provisions, arms control treaties had an added symbolic value: they recognized the Soviet Union (and later, Russia) as an equal and worthy partner to the United States and NATO, demonstrating Washington's respect for Moscow. Arms control processes are also important because they provide information about the adversary's strategic thinking, even if the negotiations themselves break down. Their absence increases the danger of new confrontations.[14]

The United States was first to challenge the value of arms control when President George W. Bush unilaterally withdrew from the Anti-Ballistic Missile (ABM) Treaty in 2002 to pursue national missile defense. The 1972 treaty was the anchor of Cold War arms control. It guaranteed that each side could deter the other by threatening a devastating nuclear strike in retaliation for any attack, and provided a definitive statement that Washington recognized Moscow's strategic parity. Soon after Bush's announcement, the United States began deploying regional ballistic missile defense (BMD) systems in Alaska and California, designed to thwart a small missile salvo from North Korea or Iran. In 2006, Bush announced that the United States would deploy a third land-based BMD system in Poland, once more against the Iranian missile threat.

In spite of consistent U.S. denials, these actions fostered a Russian perception that the United States had a hidden agenda to undercut Russia's nuclear deterrence capabilities at a time when Russia's conventional deployments were weak. The original system planned for Poland could theoretically have been used against a small number of long-range missile strikes, like those Russia might launch against the United States in a limited nuclear war. President Barack Obama attempted to reassure Russia, replacing plans for the original BMD system with land-based versions of the U.S. Aegis regional BMD systems in Romania and Poland designed to thwart only midrange and tactical rockets.[15] Most Western and Russian experts agree that the Aegis system would not be useful against Russia's huge arsenal of fast-moving intercontinental ballistic missiles unless it were drastically reconfigured.[16] Yet the theoretical possibility of such future reconfiguration left Moscow dissatisfied.[17]

NATO-led efforts since 2010 to work with Russia on a joint regional BMD system for Europe have failed.[18] Meanwhile, the 1987 Intermediate-Range Nuclear Forces (INF) Treaty may also be breaking down. The INF treaty eliminated a whole class of weapons—all land-based ballistic and cruise missiles with a range between 500 and 5,500 kilometers—from both Europe and the Russian Far East, and featured intrusive on-site inspections rather than traditional overhead satellite verification. Hard-line commentators in Moscow began to hint in 2007 that the planned U.S. BMD systems in Central Europe might force Russia to rethink the INF treaty.[19] Then, in January 2014, the United States claimed that Russia had tested a new weapon prohibited by the treaty, a ground-launched cruise missile.[20] The Kremlin reacted by arguing that Washington's land-based Aegis systems could be reconfigured to launch INF cruise missiles and thereby constituted a treaty violation. Putin has periodically threatened to withdraw from the INF treaty since then. In October 2016, the United States accused Russia of continuing to develop ground-launched cruise missiles in violation of the treaty.

Equally disturbing is the breakdown of the Treaty on Conventional Forces in Europe (CFE), which was designed to limit the number of troops and heavy conventional weapons along the central line of Cold War military confrontation. The CFE treaty had great symbolic significance. It represented Gorbachev's acceptance of a "Common European Home" reaching from the Atlantic Ocean to the Ural Mountains, and a willingness to give up long-standing Soviet Cold War plans for a surprise conventional attack on NATO. The CFE treaty had tremendous real-world effects, too: more than seventy thousand weapons systems were eliminated, more than five thousand on-site inspections were undertaken, and tens of thousands of notifications about military exercises and movements were exchanged.[21]

The CFE process began to unravel when Russian actions in Eurasia caused the United States and its allies to refuse to ratify the "adapted" CFE treaty (A/CFE) signed in 1999. The A/CFE updated the structure of the original treaty after the breakup of the Warsaw Pact and the Soviet Union, replacing bloc-to-bloc troop and weapon limits with a system of national and territorial ceilings. The sticking point in 1999 was the continued presence of Russian troops in the independent post-Soviet states of Moldova and Georgia. Russia claimed it was leading peacekeeping missions, but others saw Moscow as providing military support to client rebel regimes in violation of international law. The West accepted the presence of Russian troops as a temporary expedient because dislodging them would have risked open warfare.[22] But these Russian deployments both violated CFE member state sovereignty and allowed Russia to disperse heavy weapons abroad without oversight.

As relations with the West deteriorated, Putin announced that Russia was suspending its compliance with the CFE treaty in 2007 and forbade further weapons inspections on Russian territory.[23] Additional negotiations became politically impractical in the West after the wars in Georgia in 2008 and Ukraine in 2014, because Russia occupied territory that is internationally recognized as belonging to two CFE treaty signatories. Finally, in 2015, Russia announced that it would no longer participate in meetings of the CFE treaty's Joint Consultative Group. Although other treaty members continue to exchange data, Russia's absence means that the CFE treaty process has effectively died.

The demise of CFE has in turn left the NRFA hanging by a thread. The NRFA, which is a political agreement rather than a legally binding treaty, is the primary remaining vehicle for negotiating security cooperation between Russia and NATO. It includes a statement, originally volunteered as a unilateral pledge by the United States to assuage Russia, which is now under contention:

> NATO reiterates that in the current and foreseeable security environment, the Alliance will carry out its collective defense and other missions by ensuring the necessary interoperability, integration, and capability for reinforcement rather than by additional permanent stationing of substantial combat forces.[24]

Because this was a political pledge by NATO rather than a treaty, no technical understanding was ever reached between NATO and Russia on defining "additional permanent stationing of substantial combat forces." However, Russia has repeatedly requested that NATO provide specific numbers and demanded that all new NATO permanent forces be limited to what was agreed upon in the (unratified) A/CFE treaty in 1999: one full combat brigade of approximately five thousand soldiers for each of the new NATO members at that time (Poland, Hungary, and the Czech Republic). This would allow NATO three new brigades in total, beyond what existing NATO members held in 1997.[25] In other words, Russia believes that NATO's current twenty-eight member states should be cumulatively granted the same force limits agreed upon for nineteen states in 1999. In fact, NATO force levels have fallen so dramatically in recent years to that current deployments remain far below even what had been agreed to in 1999. The number of combat battalions located in the major Western European states had dropped from 649 in 1990 to 185 by 2015.[26] The most striking reduction was in U.S. troops: from 102,500 in 1997 to just 65,000 in 2015, of which only 33,000 are the Army forces covered by the A/CFE treaty.[27]

RUSSIA VERSUS NATO: COMPARING MILITARY CAPABILITIES

Despite Putin's current rearmament efforts, Russian conventional force deployments in Europe also remain much lower now than during the Cold War, when the Soviet Union had over 338,000 troops stationed in East Germany. For example, at the close of the Cold War, Russian battle tanks numbered over 51,000. In 2014, they totaled 2,600, well below the CFE ceiling of 20,000 tanks.[28] Yet measuring the balance between the two sides is complicated by the fact that the relative military strengths of NATO and Russia are much more ambiguous now than during the Cold War. It is impossible to make the kind of direct numerical comparisons between forces that were common then.

The NATO alliance has grown significantly, but it is unclear how well its forces would integrate their activities in wartime over what is now a much larger space. Assessing actual Russian unit strength is also a challenge. Official statements from Moscow about Russian force levels are often contradictory, and hence not useful or trustworthy. Additionally, because of demographic and conscription difficulties, some formations may be hollow, manned at partial strength.

Beyond raw numbers, estimating combat readiness for both sides is difficult. Russian successes in Ukraine and Syria have been achieved with relatively small numbers of troops and may not reflect broad capabilities across the force, especially given that Russia has struggled to find enough high-quality contract soldiers.

Similarly, beyond the United States and a few of its most stalwart allies (such as Canada, France, Germany, and the United Kingdom), it is not clear what overall NATO combat readiness levels truly are, even as various exercises try to measure them. Russian troops and weapons from outside the European region of Russia could be used for quick reinforcement in the European area. Yet NATO is not Russia's only security concern, and even the European areas of Russia may be utilized for military missions not directly related to NATO. For example, the northwestern region of Pskov is both where Russia would launch an attack on NATO member Estonia and where many of the Russian soldiers fighting in Ukraine from 2014 to 2015 were based. Russia maintains a force of around 28,000 troops distributed between Crimea and its border with Ukraine (with an additional 1,500 based in Moldova), but frequent military exercises complicate accurate troop counts.[29] NATO has used its European forces in many out-of-area operations, most recently in Afghanistan and Libya, and individual NATO members have used European bases and forces for non-NATO military interventions in Iraq, Syria, and Africa. The forces available for a Russia-NATO war would depend on whatever security challenges each side faced elsewhere. Finally, some force multipliers are not easily measurable, including the relative cyber capabilities of the two sides.

How a Crisis Might Erupt

It is impossible to predict every potential crisis that might arise between Russia and NATO member states. The Putin regime has carried out surprise actions on NATO territory in recent years that no one could reasonably have foreseen, ranging from kidnapping an Estonian security officer to hacking U.S. DNC emails.[30] The scenarios that follow, though far from exhaustive, are ones that Western experts have thought about deeply with grave concern, and are credible threats that Russian aggression may pose to NATO security.

DANGEROUS MILITARY ACTIVITIES

A crisis might inadvertently escalate after an encounter between NATO and Russian military vehicles in peacetime. Russian military aircraft and naval vessels have approached or breached NATO sovereign borders in a seemingly hostile fashion dozens of times since 2014, and have provoked dozens more dangerous incidents in international waters and airspace by coming too close at too high a speed to their U.S. and NATO counterparts.[31] (Not all of these incidents are publicly announced, so the true number may be much higher.) Any of these incidents could get out of hand and provoke a lethal response. An inkling of how such a crisis might unfold was revealed when Turkey shot down a Russian jet in November 2015 after Ankara claimed that Moscow had violated Turkey's border with Syria. Although that incident did not escalate beyond rhetoric and trade sanctions, it could have led to militarized conflict.

RUSSIAN LAND GRAB
IN OR NEAR THE BALTICS

Some Western analysts fear that a Russian military confrontation with NATO may be intentional, not inadvertent. Russia might invade the Baltic states of Estonia, Latvia, and Lithuania, either to restore control over these former Soviet territories that have been NATO member states since 2004 (and which now divide the Russian province of Kaliningrad from the rest of Russia) or simply to break the NATO alliance by demonstrating the West's inability to mount a unified response. Sweden, not a NATO member, fears that Russian aggression might extend to its strategic Baltic Sea island of Gotland and is therefore stationing permanent troops there for the first time since 2005 while increasing its cooperation with NATO.[32] An additional concern is that future instability in the former Soviet state of Belarus (also not a NATO member) might tempt Moscow to intervene militarily to restore a pro-Russian order there, provoking further tensions on NATO's Baltic borders.

In the face of NATO objections and in violation of CFE treaty understandings, Russia has conducted about a dozen unannounced military exercises in recent years designed to test troop readiness. These exercises show that Moscow is training for large-scale conventional warfare against its neighbors.[33] Russia used one such snap exercise as cover for its military intervention in Georgia in 2008 and, in theory, could do the same elsewhere. Russian military writings refer to NATO as a threat and make frequent references to the major land battles of World War II in Europe.[34]

NATO's threat perceptions were heightened when a major wargaming analysis published by the RAND Corporation in February 2016 concluded that NATO's conventional military forces would be unable to stop a surprise Russian conventional attack on Estonia and Latvia and that Moscow could occupy their capitals within sixty hours.[35] NATO reinforcements might then be blocked by a Russian attempt at antiaccess/area denial (A2/AD). Russia could use antiship missiles based in its heavily militarized Kaliningrad province to curtail NATO action in the Baltic Sea. NATO troops attempting to arrive overland would have to navigate the so-called Suwalki Gap (the narrow border connecting NATO members Poland and Lithuania), flanked by Kaliningrad on one side and Russia's sometime ally Belarus on the other.[36] Inflaming these fears are concerns that if the INF treaty crumbles, Russia could deploy nuclear-armed Iskander missiles to both Kaliningrad and Crimea.[37] Many U.S. analysts have argued that the United States and NATO need to deploy greater numbers of conventional forces in Europe to stop a growing Russian threat.[38]

DENIAL OF NATO BLACK SEA ACCESS

Russia has used its seizure of Crimea to launch the buildup and modernization of its aging Black Sea fleet and air defenses and, in summer 2016, announced that Crimea would receive sophisticated S-400 surface-to-air missiles.[39] Some analysts are concerned that Moscow might use these capabilities in an A2/AD campaign against NATO, threatening commercial Mediterranean Sea access for NATO members Romania and Bulgaria.[40]

To do so would violate the 1936 Montreux Convention that guarantees civilian ships free passage through the Bosporus and Dardanelles Straits during peacetime. It would also directly challenge Turkey's legal sovereignty over the straits at a time when Turkish-Russian relations have improved. For these reasons, this scenario is unlikely to arise out of the blue. Instead, it might be designed to deter U.S. and NATO intervention following an escalation of hostilities elsewhere along the Black Sea, such as in southern Ukraine, along the border of Russian-occupied Abkhazia with Georgia proper, or in areas of Moldova dominated by ethnic Russians. NATO has no agreed-upon policy on how to react to future Russian aggression in Eurasia that occurs near, but not in violation of, NATO borders.

RUSSIAN HYBRID WAR

The most challenging threat scenario is what NATO calls "hybrid war" and what Russia calls "information war," consisting of actions short of a full-scale invasion that are designed to be politically destabilizing. These tactics include cyberattacks, mass media disinformation and "fake news" campaigns, measures to skew popular opinion against particular local politicians or policies, and Special Operations force deception, such as clandestinely inserting provocateurs into a country to incite rioting that appears to be domestically caused. Such techniques were commonly employed by Soviet intelligence forces during the Cold War, and now internet technology expands and multiplies their effects. Rather than seeking a conventional military victory, such Russian actions "shift the onus of escalation onto NATO."[41] Instability inside a NATO member state, even when it is provoked from the outside, is not a direct military threat and therefore is not explicitly covered under Article 5 of the NATO Charter.

Russian information warfare in Ukraine is ongoing and has already occurred against NATO member states. For example, Russian state-controlled media bombards Russian speakers in the Baltics with attractive (and sometimes dishonest) pro-Moscow, anti-NATO television programming. Immense denial-of-service attacks were launched by politically motivated Russian nationalists against Estonian government websites in April 2007, when a monument commemorating Soviet forces in World War II was moved from the center of Tallinn (although the Russian state denies any involvement). Estonia acted rapidly to bolster its cyber defenses as a result, and NATO as a whole has gradually followed suit, working to develop joint cyber defense and resilience capabilities.

To undermine trust in NATO's Article 5 (and with the justification of protecting ethnic Russian populations abroad), Moscow might go further. For example, it might play on ethnic tensions in the Baltic states and encourage rioting that provokes residents of Latvia or Estonia to demand Russian peacekeeping-force assistance in a small slice of territory along the Russian border. Both states have significant ethnic Russian populations, making up 24 percent (Estonia) and 27 percent (Latvia) of their respective totals, concentrated in the capital cities and in smaller cities near the Russian border.[42] In both countries, citizenship policies for ethnic Russians have been contested, and a significant proportion of Russian-speaking residents remain officially stateless under rules set by the UN High Commissioner for Refugees: more than 91,000 in Estonia and an extraordinary 267,000 in Latvia as of 2013.[43] Some who qualify for citizenship have chosen not to receive it, and both countries have recently modified their laws to allow the younger children of stateless residents to receive automatic citizenship with parental consent.[44] Experts disagree about how satisfied Russians in Latvia and Estonia are with the current arrangement and with their broader civil rights and employment opportunities, and hence how susceptible they might be to Russian hybrid war challenges.

How to Assess and Respond to a Crisis

There is probably nothing the United States can do to stop low-level Russian information warfare and political interference in the West, except to be aware of it and call it out when it happens. Overreaction could lead to dangerous escalation. The United States would be greatly damaged by a cyber war with Russia because of the number and variety of its internet-connected civilian systems, including the growing "internet of things" in private households and public facilities such as hospitals. Because Russia plays on real political discontent in NATO countries, Western governments should track their own political vulnerabilities and address the underlying issues, including economic disappointment and ethnic tensions, that give Russian disinformation campaigns their audience appeal.

In reacting to possible military scenarios, the United States and NATO need to keep three points in mind. First, the existence of Russian plans for various scenarios does not necessarily reveal political intentions. All military organizations train for exigencies that never occur. In particular, Estonia and Latvia have enjoyed twenty-five years of political and economic freedom and Western integration, and it seems far-fetched that Russian leaders would believe they could now be easily controlled by military occupation. Second, responding to these scenarios with a NATO conventional military buildup might paradoxically increase Russian threat perceptions, making crisis escalation (and Russian contingency plan implementation) more likely. Third, Putin does have a pattern of military intervention abroad in both Ukraine and Syria, but he also has a knack for the canny bluff. Western experts disagree, for example, about how deep and sustainable the current Russian military reform and remilitarization effort really is, especially in the face of Russia's continuing economic stagnation.[45]

Then, too, the NATO rearmament that some Western analysts have called for (and even the raised European contributions to NATO finances that Trump would prefer) may be politically unfeasible in the current environment. Many EU member states who are NATO members have still not recovered from the global financial crisis of 2007 to 2008. The overall gross domestic product (GDP) of the Euro area in 2015 was lower than it had been since 2006, and that was before the United Kingdom voted to exit the EU, which threatens to darken Europe's economic outlook.[46] Although all NATO members pledge to work toward spending 2 percent of their GDP on defense, that target remains aspirational for all but a few (see figure 1). It should be noted that Estonia and Poland are among the highest contributors.

Meanwhile, the United States is increasingly focusing its own defense attention on the South China Sea and other non-European challenges, and a variety of public opinion polls show that American voters want to cut, not increase, defense spending.[47]

RECENT U.S. AND NATO MILITARY RESPONSES TO RUSSIA

In June 2014, following Russia's seizure of Crimea, President Obama launched the European Reassurance Initiative.[48] This multipronged

FIGURE 1. DEFENSE EXPENDITURE AS A SHARE OF GROSS DOMESTIC PRODUCT (BASED ON 2010 PRICES AND EXCHANGE RATES)

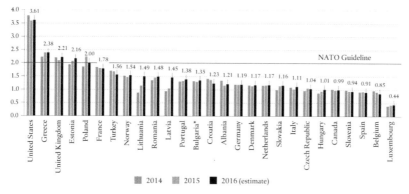

■ 2014   ■ 2015   ■ 2016 (estimate)

* Defense expenditure does not include pensions.

Source: NATO Public Diplomacy Division (July 2016).

program, originally funded through a $1 billion emergency budget initiative, was designed to showcase Washington's commitment to the defense of all NATO member states through expanded exercises and deployments. It set up a constant rotation of small U.S. Army, Air Force, and Navy units through the Baltic states and Poland. The program was continued in 2015. In early 2016, with strong bipartisan support, Obama requested congressional funding of $3.4 billion for fiscal year 2017, to begin a multiyear program now known as Operation Atlantic Resolve. The program is positioning new U.S. military equipment in Europe in the event that reinforcements are needed for a quick response to a Russian threat. The United States will also deploy several hundred personnel to staff the new missile defense site in Romania and some three hundred U.S. Marines to Norway on a trial basis this year, breaking a long-standing Norwegian tradition of prohibiting the presence of any foreign troops.[49] Meanwhile, the U.S. Army is leading the Russia New Generation Warfare Study, bringing analysts from across the government together to scrutinize Russia's actions in Ukraine for future U.S. and NATO planning.[50]

At its 2014 Wales Summit, NATO adopted a Readiness Action Plan in response to Russian challenges. Although other NATO members did not come close to matching the new U.S. commitment, the plan created new exercises, patrols, and rotational deployments that supported NATO's easternmost members, including on the Black Sea. In 2015, the size of the long-standing multinational NATO Response Force, drawn from existing deployments and designed to be ready for short-term crisis response, was tripled to forty thousand. A spearhead of five thousand troops, named the Very High Readiness Joint Task Force, also became operational in 2016, though it was widely viewed as not enough to derail determined Russian aggression.[51]

The most significant NATO actions in response to the perceived Russian threat were announced at the 2016 Warsaw Summit, envisioning the establishment over the next year of an "enhanced forward presence" in NATO's east. Four new battalions (together equivalent to approximately one new combat brigade) will be deployed. The United Kingdom will oversee a new battalion in Estonia; Canada, a battalion in Latvia; Germany, one in Lithuania; and the United States, one in Poland, where this new multinational division will be headquartered.[52] Although details have not been made public, reportedly each new battalion will include around one thousand troops.[53] NATO also expressed some support for Romania's ideas about a new multinational Black Sea maritime presence but announced no new NATO deployments there. Furthermore, at its 2014 Wales Summit, NATO had declared that cyber defense was part of its collective defense planning, and, at the Warsaw Summit, current Secretary General Jens Stoltenberg affirmed that cyberspace is an operational domain of conflict, potentially making way for member states with offensive cyber programs (including the United States, France, the Netherlands, and the United Kingdom) to use such weapons on NATO's behalf.[54]

The force increases envisioned in the Warsaw Summit are far below the recommendations of more hawkish Western defense analysts. But they do establish persistent multinational forces near Russia's borders and are a strong symbol of NATO's deterrent tripwire. When capable allies—such as the United States, the United Kingdom, Germany, and Canada—demonstrate that they are willing to put themselves in harm's way to answer an outside attack, it sends a strong signal that the alliance will hold. Recent enhanced NATO military cooperation with nearby neutral states, including Sweden and Finland, has also helped demonstrate a unified Western deterrent.

The focus on a tripwire strategy is not new or radical for NATO; it has a long historical precedent. To deter the Soviet Union, NATO never relied on matching its superior conventional forces and surprise attack capabilities during the Cold War. NATO countries historically—and successfully—relied instead on what were called offset strategies: the threat early in the Cold War to use nuclear weapons to stop a Soviet conventional attack on Western Europe, and later to use U.S. advanced weaponry for stealthy and precisely targeted long-distance strikes against Soviet targets.[55] Strategic planners on the Russian general staff received education and training from their Soviet counterparts, and many Russian generals today began their careers as junior officers in Soviet times. They know this history. They know that neither Russia nor any other state comes close to being a peer competitor against the overwhelmingly powerful U.S. military. Most important, they are likely to be similarly rational actors, with no desire to start a war that would eventually destroy Russia.

Recommendations

To make military crises less likely to arise, but to prepare for meeting them if they do, the Trump administration should work with Washington's NATO partners to prioritize three intertwined policy commitments.

First, the Trump administration should continue to work with its NATO allies to deter Russia from threatening or undermining any NATO member. Deterrence can succeed not merely by threatening a punishing response to Russian aggression, as the most extreme measures of a tripwire strategy would entail, but also through simultaneous "deterrence by denial"—by making Russian aggression so costly, and with so few perceived benefits, that it is not worth pursuing.

Second, the Trump administration should take reasonable actions alongside its NATO allies to reassure Russian political and military officials and the Russian public that the United States and NATO have defensive intentions and do not threaten Russian territory. The United States cannot stop Putin's propaganda or overcome all deep-seated Russian suspicions about the West, but Congress should support Trump's efforts to invalidate the image of the United States as Russia's enemy that Putin has presented to his people. While it might appear that a commitment to reassure is in tension with the commitment to deter, in fact they can work together as a defensive strategy to make Europe more stable.

A third commitment will help bring deterrence and reassurance into harmony: policy decisions should be based on consistent, transparent, rule-based criteria wherever possible. Law-abiding behavior will deflect Russian accusations of hypocrisy, and the United States will have an easier time uniting with its European allies to achieve shared aims if it shows that it continues to respect international law and institutions.

DETERRENCE MEASURES

- **Reaffirm the U.S. commitment to NATO defense.** President Trump should immediately reaffirm, and the State Department and the Pentagon should periodically restate, that the defense of all NATO member states is Washington's highest priority in Europe and an ongoing legal commitment because of the NATO Charter. This is especially important because many NATO allies interpreted some of Trump's statements during the campaign and in early 2017 as implying that the U.S. commitment to NATO is in doubt.

- **Prioritize fulfillment of 2016 Warsaw Summit force pledges, while emphasizing their legitimacy under the 1999 A/CFE agreement.** To demonstrate this commitment to NATO, the president and the Pentagon should prioritize sustaining the newly deployed U.S. enhanced forward presence battalion to Poland, and urge Canadian, British, and German allies to quickly deploy and sustain their parallel commitments to lead new battalions in the Baltics. The Trump administration should emphasize that these new deployments are far lower than what Russia itself agreed to as being legitimate in 1999, but that they establish a visible symbol of NATO cohesion and a tripwire against aggression. The president, the Pentagon, and the State Department should also emphasize that other small new U.S. deployments (including at the Romanian missile defense site and in Norway) are legitimate, ongoing, defensive symbols of Washington's commitment to Europe's security. Because current plans for these deployments involve relocation rather than new hiring, the financial costs will be relatively limited.

- **Rely on comprehensive capabilities, not just conventional military forces, to deter Russia in the European theater.** Public statements by defense officials should make clear that the Pentagon need not match Russian conventional deployments to fulfill its deterrent promise, just as NATO never matched Soviet conventional forces in Europe. The United States currently has 1,367 nuclear warheads deployed on strategic missile, submarine, and bomber forces, ready for use at a moment's notice, so its nuclear deterrent against Russia remains intact. While some specifics of the historical offset strategies are dated, current and future planning should rely on similarly asymmetrical responses, not an expensive and destabilizing conventional arms buildup in Europe.

- **Publicize U.S. reliance on comprehensive, asymmetrical capabilities for deterrence.** To deter effectively, especially across domains of action, U.S. planners should communicate the basic outlines of their strategic thinking and reaffirm the appropriateness and proportionality of potential responses under international law.[56] The goal is to achieve the same delicate balance that was the focus of Cold War nuclear planning, whereby Russian planners are left so apprehensive about the potential consequences of aggression that they are deterred, but not so worried about U.S. intentions that they strike preemptively.

- **Think creatively about what cross-domain deterrence, or using capabilities in one domain (such as air, land, cyber, or even trade and finance) to deter threats in another, as well as deterrence by denial can mean today.** The following recommendations on cyber activities, sanctions, and political reforms in the Baltics are examples of such thinking but should not be taken as the only possible choices.

  - **Continue to build U.S. offensive battlefield cyber capabilities and encourage NATO partners in similar efforts.** President Trump has announced that a Pentagon cyber-defense strategy is a high priority for his administration. Offensive battlefield cyber measures, designed to thwart an air, land, or sea attack by disrupting an enemy's military C4I (command, control, communication, computer, and intelligence) capabilities should be prioritized in his comprehensive cyber plan. The unknowability of the reach of U.S. and allied battlefield cyber technology—which could, for example, send an invading force toward an incorrect target, leave a unit cut off from its headquarters, or disable battlefield air defense radars—raises the risks and costs of Russian military intervention against NATO territory beyond what a conventional response alone would accomplish. Yet cyber technology is often ignored in war-gaming exercises that lead to demands for a NATO conventional force buildup. Russia has already demonstrated its ability and willingness to use cyber weapons and has publicized its own battlefield cyber planning. It is therefore unlikely that increased Western attention to battlefield cyber offense would spark new instability, since Russian programs are progressing regardless of Western actions.

  - **Create a "cyber incubator" policy to encourage partnership between the U.S. government and the private sector.** U.S. Cyber Command's current 133-member team faces a particular challenge in hiring new talent, given the much higher salaries available in

Silicon Valley. President Trump should create a "cyber incubator," allowing experts to cycle in and out of Cyber Command service from the private sector for stints of one to two years, while forgiving student loan debt for those choosing Cyber Command service.[57] Since the primary cost of cyber weapons is the people who build them and their intellectual capital, creating expert synergy across the private/public divide would reduce long-term costs.[58] Strengthening cyber capabilities and implementing new staffing measures would improve the United States' extended deterrence in Europe and maximize the comparative advantage of its vibrant private cybersecurity sector.

– **Encourage the establishment of NATO-country cyber embassies on foreign soil to enhance deterrence through denial.** In formal and informal discussions with representatives from Latvia, Poland, and other NATO members concerned about Russian information warfare, President Trump and Pentagon officials should push for the adoption of cyber embassies, following the model laid out by Estonia. Partnering with Microsoft, the Estonian government is working to create a data services mirror in an alternative NATO member state that will allow Estonian government functions, citizen services, and official data integrity (for example, property records) to continue unabated in the event of a massive cyberattack or military occupation.[59] This can make both cyber war and land seizures in the Baltics less profitable for Russia and therefore less enticing as a military option.

– **Prepare a broad menu of graduated sanctions as a cross-domain deterrence tool.** The Trump administration should not eliminate the possibility of using sanctions against Russia in the future. The Treasury, State, and Justice Departments have gained multilateral support and global compliance with recent financial sanctions policies against Iran, Russia, and other countries, including even China's tacit acquiescence.[60] Russia should remain on notice that in the event of attack on a NATO country, including a damaging cyberattack against civilian infrastructure, the United States and its allies are prepared to impose new sanctions that could be escalated against individuals, companies, banks, or entire industries, limiting access to capital markets, finance, insurance, technology, or financial systems such as the Society for Worldwide Interbank Financial Telecommunication (SWIFT).[61] Although sanctions would affect

U.S. trade and investment sectors unevenly, they are a relatively inexpensive tool. U.S. exports of goods to Russia in 2015 were valued at just over $7 billion, and imports from Russia were valued at $16.4 billion, a drop in the bucket of the trillions of dollars of U.S. foreign trade. U.S. direct investments in Russia were valued at $9.2 billion in 2015, again a small fraction of its $5 trillion overall foreign direct investments. And though the cost to some NATO allies would be much higher, a direct Russian attack on NATO territory would likely shift allied political considerations toward cooperation with U.S. leadership on sanctions policy.

– **Encourage the resolution of ethnic political tensions in Estonia and Latvia as an example of deterrence by denial.** Because language and citizenship policies are often flashpoints for ethnic tension, finding inclusive compromises will decrease the attractiveness to Russia of trying to stir up trouble in the Baltics. Political actions can serve as a form of deterrence through denial, by delegitimizing and thereby outing as provocations any Russian efforts to incite rioting or demands for the deployment of peacekeeping troops. President Trump and the State Department should use formal and informal discussions to encourage Estonia and Latvia to better integrate their Russian populations. Both countries have made real progress in this respect over past decades, partly in response to international pressure. But more could be done, both by offering unconditional citizenship to a greater share of stateless residents born after the collapse of the Soviet Union in 1991 and by expanding employment opportunities and empathetic community policing efforts.

• **Encourage NATO in its planning scenarios to include consideration of how the alliance would react to potential new Russian land grabs beyond NATO borders.** New Russian aggression in southern Ukraine or Georgia, in Russian-speaking areas of Moldova, in Belarus, in other post-Soviet states like Kazakhstan, or in Sweden (namely, its Gotland Province) might be designed at least in part to break NATO by sowing confusion about how to respond. The State Department and the Pentagon should work with allies to discuss possible scenarios and map out gradations of possible joint reactions to Russian aggression. This could prevent such a Russian surprise from derailing the alliance, and could also deter Russia from the belief that engaging in such actions would cause the alliance to collapse in confusion.

REASSURANCE MEASURES

- **Treat Russian leaders and the Russian state with respect.** Trump's initial comments about Putin have been complimentary. He is unlikely to replicate anytime soon Obama's insulting 2013 statement that Putin seemed "like the bored kid in the back of the classroom" or 2014 characterization of Russia as a "regional power" (thereby dismissing Russia's nuclear reach and UN veto), or former Secretary of State Hillary Clinton's 2014 comparison of Putin to Hitler.[62] But Trump is proud of making surprising and unvarnished comments in tweets and interviews. Even when U.S. interactions with Russia hit inevitable bumps, the Trump administration will achieve more if it remains diplomatic and unemotional, and helps Russian leaders save face at home.

- **Formally reaffirm President Trump's message that the United States does not seek to impose "regime change" on Russia, while holding Putin accountable if he will not reciprocate, by tying this message to a new accord on limiting offensive cyber action against civilians in peacetime.** In his inaugural address, Trump said: "We do not seek to impose our way of life on anyone." He should communicate the idea that avoiding a U.S. government crusade against the Russian regime serves U.S. and allied geopolitical interests. Members of the Trump administration and Congress should similarly accept that the United States has a limited ability to influence Russia's internal political development, that Putin fears Western attempts to create regime change in Russia above all else, that these fears helped motivate Putin's offensive cyber interference in the 2016 U.S. election, and that Putin's worries undermine efforts to achieve stability in Europe. This does not mean that the United Sates cannot hold Putin accountable for Russian actions against the West—for example, by placing further sanctions against the Putin regime if Moscow does not forswear future "information war" interference in U.S. and other NATO countries' domestic politics. To encourage reciprocity, the Trump administration should propose a cyber weapon limitation agreement with Putin, whereby each side agrees not to publicize emails and other data gained from hacking civilians in peacetime—and where violations reliably attributed to the Russian state are punished. Punishment could take the form of official publicity and condemnation of Russian violations, designed to undermine international trust in Moscow and hence Russia's ability to enter into other international agreements. It could also take the form of additional sanctions. As the United States is more vulnerable to escalatory activity in cyberspace, retaliation to Russian hacking through offensive cyber action should be considered only as a last resort.

- **Reaffirm the U.S. desire to maintain the NRFA.** Some commentators have recommended shaming Russia for its aggression in Ukraine by declaring the NRFA null and void, given that it is based on principles of human rights and sovereignty recognition. But such a declaration would accomplish little and destroy the last remaining institutional framework for security cooperation with Russia in Europe. Even if Russia publicly disavows the NRFA, the State Department should continue to emphasize that the NRFA remains its preferred cornerstone of NATO-Russia relations. The United States and NATO should abrogate the NRFA only if Russia takes military or other seriously damaging action against a European NATO member state.

- **Work with allies to publicly clarify NATO's understanding of its NRFA pledge of no "additional permanent stationing of substantial combat forces."** NATO leaders—including the U.S. ambassador to NATO and other officials at NATO headquarters—should push the alliance to increase the transparency of its interpretation of this pledge even while maintaining flexibility in absolute numbers for future negotiations with Russia. For example, NATO muddied the waters at its 2016 Warsaw Summit by calling its new deployments "rotating" battalions rather than clearly stating that they represent new long-term deployments that are consistent with the NRFA pledge. Although a clarification will likely not assuage the Putin regime, it will boost the credibility of the alliance at home and undercut Russian propaganda efforts in the Baltics and elsewhere to portray reasonable new NATO deployments as aggressive.

- **Support new conventional military deployments in Europe only up to the limit of NATO's internal understanding of the 1999 A/CFE treaty requirements, unless Russia invades or seriously damages a NATO member state.** The administration should work with its NATO allies to clarify that NATO has never accepted Russia's demand for a three-brigade ceiling on an enlarged alliance's total future deployments, but that it will limit its geographical flank deployments to retain consistency with the spirit of the CFE treaty process. NATO is right to argue that the A/CFE ceiling agreed upon for nineteen members in 1999 should not be the limit for the twenty-eight allies today that span a much larger border with Russia. But no reasonable interpretation of the NRFA would permit what was suggested in the 2016 RAND study, of four additional brigades deployed to NATO's northeastern flank on top of existing Baltics deployment levels. The Trump administration should firmly reiterate this position to both domestic critics and Central and East European allies who may push for more. This should not be read as a concession to Russia, since NATO need not match Russian conventional force levels to deter Russian military action, and a NATO buildup might actually harm its own security.

- **Publicly state that the United States believes Ukraine does not currently meet NATO membership standards and has a long way to go.** While the precise standards for NATO membership accession are complex and worked out by NATO as a whole with each applicant state, there is a set of basic, agreed-upon political, economic, and security principles that new members must address, and Ukraine is at present far from meeting them.[63] The criteria are designed to ensure that new members strengthen the alliance, rather than embroil NATO in unnecessary conflicts. Russian officials have stated that the prospect of NATO membership for Ukraine was one of the primary drivers of Moscow's annexation of Crimea and its naval port of Sevastopol. An official State Department restatement of these NATO membership criteria would help reassure Russia about the limits of NATO enlargement while encouraging Ukrainian society to do more to move the country on the path of stable democratic development. Ukraine need not be a NATO member to receive support from the United States and other NATO countries.

- **Explicitly tie the planned deployment of U.S. interceptor missiles at the land-based Aegis BMD system in Poland to Iran's behavior in fulfilling its commitments to the nuclear nonproliferation deal reached in 2015 (the Joint Comprehensive Plan of Action).** Ground has been broken and installation of electronic equipment has begun at the new BMD site in Redzikowo, Poland, but the interceptor system is not scheduled for full deployment until 2018. To demonstrate that this BMD system is indeed designed against a threat from Iran and not Russia, the United States should reach an agreement with Poland that missiles will be stored on U.S. territory and

deployed to Poland only if Iran appears to be violating the terms of
the agreement or achieving breakout (that is, production of enough
weapons-grade nuclear material to make one nuclear weapon). The
Trump administration should therefore accept and maintain the current Iran nuclear deal, which Russia helped design, as a means of con-
tributing to stability in Europe.

- **Encourage new subregional bilateral and multilateral agreements on limiting dangerous military incidents between NATO
and other European states and Russia, especially in the Baltic and
Nordic regions.** Russia has clearly not kept to the bilateral agreements the Soviet Union made with the United States in 1972 and 1989
on limiting dangerous military incidents at sea and in the air. But the
Pentagon should work with allies to explore and champion additional
subregional negotiations on dangerous military activities as a way to
keep communications channels open even at a time of distrust, and to
test Russian intentions. The Trump administration should also work
with Congress to lift recently enacted legal limits on U.S.-Russian
military-to-military contacts, to allow informal discussion of such
agreements at lower levels.

- **Work with NATO allies to eventually reestablish regional arms
control negotiations on both conventional and nuclear weapons.**
If relatively narrow military-to-military dangerous-incident agreements prove workable, it would be a sign that Moscow might genuinely be receptive to reopening larger arms control negotiations. At
some future point, the State Department and the Pentagon might
work with NATO allies to support a Baltic region treaty to limit weapons and troops along each side of Russia's northwestern borders (the
Baltic countries are not CFE members), and perhaps even a treaty
process focused on regional missile defense. At the moment, the
chances of making progress in either of these broader areas appears
miniscule: negotiations would squander both domestic and foreign
political capital unless relations with Russia warm significantly.
Nonetheless, the State Department should keep these possibilities
on the table, and publicly treat smaller-scale dangerous military activities agreements the Pentagon might negotiate as first steps.

Conclusion

As a candidate, Donald J. Trump cast doubt on the U.S. commitment to NATO. Now, even as he pursues new cooperation with Russia, President Trump will need to demonstrate through his words and actions that his administration actually prioritizes NATO and the U.S. role in its defense at a time of continuing Russian hostility toward the United States' oldest and most reliable alliance. NATO forces and institutions assist U.S. security efforts at a global level, and a peaceful, democratic Europe helps protect U.S. values and interests. An increasingly aggressive Russia challenges NATO's current security perceptions, and may at some future point jeopardize NATO's territorial integrity. The breakdown of arms control heightens the danger. A variety of military crises are imaginable that could lead to escalation.

Some congressional leaders and prominent U.S. analysts trying to sway the Trump administration have portrayed the situation as a one-sided Russian threat, but Washington should recognize that past U.S. and NATO indifference toward a weakened post–Cold War Russia helped create the current threat environment. Most important, the Trump administration should recognize that the unknowability of Russian intentions means that the United States and NATO are faced with a dilemma: being too aggressive could provoke Russian fears and lead to a militarized crisis, but being too passive could tempt Russia to take military action in the belief that it would be unopposed.

The Trump administration needs to demonstrate strength and deter Russia from threatening NATO, while working with allies to reassure Russia to whatever degree is practicable about NATO's own defensive intentions. This can be done at relatively low cost. Greatly expanded conventional force deployments would be unduly provocative and are unnecessary, given the U.S. and allied enhanced forward presence tripwire in Europe, as well as U.S. and NATO offset strategy capabilities in cyberspace and through sanctions. Deterrence by denial should also be strengthened by encouraging continued ethnic inclusion in Latvia and Estonia.

The most important deterrent actions that the Trump administration should immediately take are to prioritize, support, and publicly justify the deployment of the enhanced forward presence forces already promised by the United States and its allies at NATO's 2016 Warsaw summit; to build and publicize U.S. Cyber Command's battlefield offensive capabilities while encouraging NATO allies in their own battlefield cyber and cyber defense efforts; and to avoid forswearing the use of future sanctions against Russia.

The most important reassurance actions the Trump administration should immediately take are to emphasize the U.S. desire to maintain the NRFA and the U.S. belief that Ukraine is not yet ready for NATO membership. Trump should also immediately declare that the United States is not pursuing regime change against Russia, while proposing a pact of mutual non-interference in each other's domestic political systems. Military-to-military negotiations with Russia on avoiding dangerous military activities should be opened over the course of the next year. In the coming years, if military-to-military negotiations succeed, then expansion of arms control efforts in Europe should also become a high priority.

President Trump and his advisors should also take pains to always speak respectfully and diplomatically about Russian leaders and the Russian state, even when the inevitable frustrations of the relationship might make an offhand dismissive remark or tweet seem tempting. Wise policy choices can protect U.S. interests in Europe now and create the basis for a more cooperative relationship in the future, if Russian elites decide to alter Moscow's recent hostile trajectory.

Endnotes

1. Alina Polyakova, "Why Europe Is Right to Fear Putin's Useful Idiots," ForeignPolicy .com, February 23, 2016.
2. For example, see Neil MacFarquhar, "How Russians Pay to Play in Other Countries," *New York Times*, December 30, 2016.
3. For excellent histories of this process, see Martin A. Smith, "A Bumpy Road to an Unknown Destination? NATO-Russia relations, 1991–2002," European Security 11, no. 4 (2002): 59–77; Angela Stent, *The Limits of Partnership: U.S.-Russian Relations in the Twenty-First Century* (Princeton, NJ: Princeton University Press, 2014).
4. Strobe Talbott, *The Russia Hand: A Memoir of Presidential Diplomacy* (New York: Random House, 2003).
5. Talbott, *Russia Hand*.
6. Andrei Kortunov, "NATO Enlargement and Russia: In Search of an Adequate Response," in *Will NATO Go East? The Debate over Enlarging the Atlantic Alliance*, ed. David C. Haglund (Kingston: Queen's University Centre for International Relations, 1996), pp. 71–72.
7. Marcus Warren, "Putin Lets NATO 'Recruit' in Baltic," *The Independent*, June 25, 2002.
8. Lincoln A. Mitchell, *Uncertain Democracy: U.S. Foreign Policy and Georgia's Rose Revolution* (Philadelphia: University of Pennsylvania Press, 2008), p. 117; Andrew Wilson, "Ukraine's Orange Revolution, NGOs and the Role of the West," *Cambridge Review of International Affairs* 19, no. 1 (March 2006): 21–32.
9. North Atlantic Council, Bucharest Summit Declaration, April 3, 2008, http://www .nato.int/cps/en/natolive/official_texts_8443.htm.
10. Anne Gearan, "In Recording of U.S. Diplomat, Blunt Talk on Ukraine," *Washington Post*, February 6, 2014.
11. Stephen R. Covington, "The Culture of Strategic Thought Behind Russia's Modern Approach to Warfare," Harvard Kennedy School Belfer Center Defense and Intelligence Projects Paper, October 2016.
12. Kimberly Marten, "Informal Political Networks and Putin's Foreign Policy: The Examples of Iran and Syria," *Problems of Post-Communism* 62, no. 2 (Summer 2015): 71–87.
13. Ekaterina Grobman, "Inside the Power Struggle Within the Russian Elite," *Russia Direct*, August 5, 2016.
14. William J. Perry, *My Journey at the Nuclear Brink* (Stanford, CA: Stanford University Press, 2015), p. 53.
15. Although the original plan had been to deploy systems in Poland and the Czech Republic, the first Aegis Ashore system was opened in Romania in May 2016. Plans are to open another in Poland in 2018.
16. Jaganath Sankaran, "Missile Defense Against Iran Without Threatening Russia," *Arms Control Today*, November 4, 2013; NATO Deputy Secretary General Alexander

Vershbow, "The Future of Missile Defence: A NATO Perspective," address to the Institute for National Security Studies (INSS) Missile Defence Conference, Israel, January 15, 2014, http://www.nato.int/cps/en/natohq/opinions_106142.htm.

17. Keir Giles with Andrew Monaghan, *European Missile Defense and Russia* (Carlisle, PA: U.S. Army War College Strategic Studies Institute, July 2014).

18. Vershbow, "Future of Missile Defense."

19. These views are summarized by Alexei Arbatov, "Missile Defense and the Intermediate Nuclear Forces Treaty," paper commissioned by the International Commission on Nuclear Non-proliferation and Disarmament, Canberra, March 2009.

20. For background, see Steven Pifer, "The Moscow Missile Mystery: Is Russia Actually Violating the INF Treaty?," Brookings Institution, January 31, 2014; Amy F. Woolf, *Russian Compliance with the Intermediate Range Nuclear Forces (INF) Treaty: Background and Issues for Congress* (Washington, DC: Congressional Research Service, April 2016).

21. Both these numbers and the history that follows are taken from Janet Andres, "CFE: Will It Remain a Cornerstone of European Security?" American Diplomacy (U.S. Foreign Service), September 2007.

22. Dov Lynch, *Russian Peacekeeping Strategies in the CIS: The Cases of Moldova, Georgia and Tajikistan* (New York: St. Martins, 2000).

23. Wade Boese, "Russia Unflinching on CFE Treaty Suspension," *Arms Control Today*, June 11, 2008.

24. William Alberque, "'Substantial Combat Forces' in the Context of NATO-Russia Relations," Research Paper 131 (Rome: NATO Defense College Research Division, June 2016).

25. Wolfgang Richter, "Sub-Regional Arms Control for the Baltics: What Is Desirable? What Is Feasible?" Deep Cuts Working Paper 8 (July 2016), pp. 12–13; German-Russian-U.S. Deep Cuts Commission, "Back From the Brink: Toward Restraint and Dialogue Between Russia and the West," University of Hamburg Institute for Peace Research and Security Policy, June 2016, p. 12.

26. International Institute of Strategic Studies (IISS), "Comparative Defense Statistics," *The Military Balance* 116, no. 1: 24.

27. IISS, "United States," *The Military Balance* 98, no. 1: 27; Andrew Tilghman, "More U.S. Troops Deploying to Europe in 2017," *Military Times*, February 2, 2016; Kathleen H. Hicks, Heather A. Conley, et al., *Evaluating Future U.S. Army Force Posture in Europe, Phase I Report* (Washington, DC: Center for Strategic and International Studies, February 2016).

28. For comparison, see the data provided by IISS, *The Military Balance*, "Russia," vol. 92 (1992) and vol. 116 (2016), and especially the data included in the pull-out chart on Russia, "Force Comparison 1990–91 and 2014," *The Military Balance* vol. 115 (2015), print edition.

29. For example, a March 2016 offensive exercise included 33,000 Russian troops near Finland, Norway, and Sweden, and an October 2016 exercise in Pskov, near the Estonian border, involved 5,000 Russian troops.

30. U.S. Department of Homeland Security, "Joint Statement from the Department of Homeland Security and Office of the Director of National Intelligence on Election Security," October 7, 2016.

31. The European Leadership Network cataloged more than sixty incidents between March 2014 and March 2015 alone. See Ian Kearns and Denitsa Raynova, "Managing Dangerous Incidents: The Need for a NATO-Russia Memorandum of Understanding," European Leadership Network, March 7, 2016.

32. Richard Milne, "Sweden Sends Troops to Baltic Island amid Russia Tensions," *Financial Times*, March 12, 2015.

33. Johan Norberg, *Training to Fight: Russia's Major Military Exercises, 2011–2014* (Stockholm: Swedish Defense Research Agency, 2016).

34. Aleksandr V. Rogovoy and Keir Giles, *A Russian View on Landpower* (Carlisle, PA: U.S. Army War College, Strategic Studies Institute, 2015).

35. David A. Shlapak and Michael W. Johnson, *Reinforcing Deterrence on NATO's Eastern Flank: Wargaming the Defense of the Baltics* (Santa Monica, CA: RAND Arroyo Center, 2016).

36. Agnia Grigas, "NATO's Vulnerable Link in Europe: Poland's Suwalki Gap," *NATO-Source*, February 9, 2016.

37. Andrew Osborn, "Russia Seen Putting New Nuclear-Capable Missiles Along NATO Border by 2019," Reuters, June 23, 2016.

38. R. Reed Anderson, Patrick J. Ellis, Antonio M. Paz, Kyle A. Reed, Lendy "Alamo" Renegar, and John T. Vaughan, *Strategic Landpower and a Resurgent Russia: An Operational Approach to Deterrence* (Carlisle, PA: U.S. Army War College, May 2016); Hicks and Conley, *Evaluating Future U.S. Army Force Posture in Europe*; Jeffrey A. Stacey, "Restoring Conventional Deterrence in Europe: How to Climb Out of the Joint Security Trap," *NATOSource*, May 6, 2016; Gen. Sir Richard Shirreff and Maciej Olex-Szczytowski, "Arming for Deterrence: How Poland and NATO Should Counter a Resurgent Russia," Atlantic Council Report, July 2016.

39. Robert Coalson, "News Analysis: Russian Buildup Focuses Concerns around the Black Sea," Radio Free Europe/Radio Liberty, February 23, 2016.

40. Janusz Bugajski and Peter Doran, "Black Sea Defended," Strategic Report 2, Center for European Policy Analysis, July 2016.

41. James J. Wirtz, "Cyber War and Strategic Culture: The Russian Integration of Cyber Power into Grand Strategy," in *Cyber War in Perspective: Russian Aggression against Ukraine*, ed. Kenneth Geers (Tallinn: NATO Cooperative Cyber Defense Center of Excellence, 2015), p. 34.

42. Agnia Grigas, "Russia's Motives in the Baltic States," Foreign Policy Research Institute E-notes, December 2015.

43. "Stateless Persons," United Nations High Commissioner for Refugees, 2013, p. 41.

44. Government of Estonia, "Citizenship," http://estonia.eu/about-estonia/society/citizenship.html.

45. Roger N. McDermott, *The Reform of Russia's Conventional Armed Forces* (Washington, DC: Jamestown Foundation, 2011); McDermott, "Putin Bluffs on Challenging NATO," *Eurasia Daily Monitor* 13, no. 116, June 28, 2016; McDermott, "Russia's Futuristic Military Plagued by Old Problems," *Eurasia Daily Monitor* 13, no. 138, July 29, 2016.

46. World Bank, "Global Daily: Euro Area GDP Growth in First Quarter Revised Down," May 13, 2016.

47. Lauren Chadwick, "Most Voters Favor Defense Cuts. Most Politicians Don't," Time.com, March 10, 2016.

48. This paragraph is drawn from Mark F. Cancian and Lisa Sawyer Samp, "The European Reassurance Initiative," Center for Strategic and International Studies, February 9, 2016.

49. Bugajski and Doran, "Black Sea Defended"; "US Troops to Be Stationed in Norway in Break With Tradition," BBC News, October 25, 2016.

50. Bryan Bender, "The Secret U.S. Army Study that Targets Moscow," *Politico*, April 14, 2016.

51. "NATO Response Force," North Atlantic Treaty Organization, June 23, 2016; Sam Jones, "NATO Rapid Unit Not Fit for Eastern Europe Deployment, Say Generals," *Financial Times*, May 15, 2016.

52. North Atlantic Council, Warsaw Summit Communiqué, July 9, 2016, http://www
.nato.int/cps/en/natohq/official_texts_133169.htm.

53. James Stavridis, "The NATO Summit's Winners and Losers," ForeignPolicy.com,
July 11, 2016.

54. National Cyber Security Centre, *Cyber Security Assessment Netherlands 2015: Cross-
Border Cyber Security Approach Necessary*, Netherlands Ministry of Security and Justice, November 15, 2015; James Blitz, "UK Becomes First State to Admit to Offensive
Cyber Attack Capability," *Financial Times*, September 29, 2013; Joseph Fitsanakis,
"France's Ex-Cyber Spy Chief Speaks Candidly About Hacking Operations," Intelnews
.org, September 16, 2016; and Herb Lin, "NATO's Designation of Cyber as an Operational Domain of Conflict," Lawfare, June 15, 2016.

55. Perry, *My Journey at the Nuclear Brink*, pp. 33–38.

56. Vincent Manzo, "Deterrence and Escalation in Cross-domain Operations: Where Do
Space and Cyberspace Fit?" National Defense University Strategic Forum No. 272,
December 2011, http://ndupress.ndu.edu/Portals/68/Documents/stratforum/SF-272
.pdf.

57. Steven Weber and Betsy Cooper, "Cybersecurity Policy Ideas for a New Presidency,"
University of California Berkeley Center for Long-Term Cybersecurity November 18,
2016, https://cltc.berkeley.edu/files/2016/11/Center_for_Long_Term_Cybersecurity
.pdf.

58. Max Smeets, "How Much Does a Cyber Weapon Cost? Nobody Knows," *Net Politics*,
November 21, 2016.

59. Possibilities discussed include the UK and Luxembourg. See Kevin Townsend, "Estonia's 'Data Embassy' Could be UK's First Brexit Cyber Casualty," *Security Week*,
August 10, 2016.

60. Alexander Gabuev, "Did Western Sanctions Affect Sino-Russian Economic Ties?"
China Policy Institute Blog, April 26, 2016.

61. Henry Farrell, "Russia Is Hinting at a New Cold War over SWIFT. So What's SWIFT?"
Monkey Cage blog, January 28, 2015.

62. Steve Holland and Margaret Chadbourn, "Obama Describes Putin as 'Like a Bored
Kid,'" Reuters, August 9, 2013; Scott Wilson, "Obama Dismisses Russia as 'Regional
Power' Acting out of Weakness," *Washington Post*, March 25, 2014; Philip Rucker,
"Hillary Clinton Says Putin's Actions Are Like 'What Hitler Did Back in the '30s,'"
Washington Post, March 5, 2014.

63. These were first laid out by Hans Binnendijk, "NATO Can't Be Vague About Commitment to Eastern Europe," *International Herald Tribune*, November 8, 1991. During
the administration of Bill Clinton, it was Defense Secretary William Perry who
became their "guardian." George W. Grayson, *Strange Bedfellows: NATO Marches East*
(Lanham, MD: University Press of America, 1999), p. 72.

About the Author

Kimberly Marten is the Ann Whitney Olin professor of political science at Barnard College and a faculty member of the Graduate School of Arts and Sciences and the School of International and Public Affairs at Columbia University. She directs the program on U.S.-Russia Relations at Columbia's Harriman Institute. She has written four books, including, most recently, *Warlords: Strong-Arm Brokers in Weak States.* Her first book, *Engaging the Enemy: Organization Theory and Soviet Military Innovation,* won the Marshall Shulman Prize.

Advisory Committee for
Reducing Tensions Between Russia and NATO

This report reflects the judgments and recommendations of the authors. It does not necessarily represent the views of members of the advisory committee, whose involvement should in no way be interpreted as an endorsement of the report by either themselves or the organizations with which they are affiliated.

Mission Statement
of the Center for Preventive Action

The Center for Preventive Action (CPA) seeks to help prevent, defuse, or resolve deadly conflicts around the world and to expand the body of knowledge on conflict prevention. It does so by creating a forum in which representatives of governments, international organizations, nongovernmental organizations, corporations, and civil society can gather to develop operational and timely strategies for promoting peace in specific conflict situations. The center focuses on conflicts in countries or regions that affect U.S. interests, but may be otherwise overlooked; where prevention appears possible; and when the resources of the Council on Foreign Relations can make a difference. The center does this by

- Issuing Council Special Reports to evaluate and respond rapidly to developing conflict situations and formulate timely, concrete policy recommendations that the U.S. government, international community, and local actors can use to limit the potential for deadly violence.
- Engaging the U.S. government and news media in conflict prevention efforts. CPA staff members meet with administration officials and members of Congress to brief on CPA's findings and recommendations; facilitate contacts between U.S. officials and important local and external actors; and raise awareness among journalists of potential flashpoints around the globe.
- Building networks with international organizations and institutions to complement and leverage the Council's established influence in the U.S. policy arena and increase the impact of CPA's recommendations.
- Providing a source of expertise on conflict prevention to include research, case studies, and lessons learned from past conflicts that policymakers and private citizens can use to prevent or mitigate future deadly conflicts.

Council Special Reports

Published by the Council on Foreign Relations

Afghanistan After the Drawdown
Seth G. Jones and Keith Crane; CSR No. 67, November 2013
A Center for Preventive Action Report

The Future of U.S. Special Operations Forces
Linda Robinson; CSR No. 66, April 2013

Reforming U.S. Drone Strike Policies
Micah Zenko; CSR No. 65, January 2013
A Center for Preventive Action Report

Countering Criminal Violence in Central America
Michael Shifter; CSR No. 64, April 2012
A Center for Preventive Action Report

Saudi Arabia in the New Middle East
F. Gregory Gause III; CSR No. 63, December 2011
A Center for Preventive Action Report

Partners in Preventive Action: The United States and International Institutions
Paul B. Stares and Micah Zenko; CSR No. 62, September 2011
A Center for Preventive Action Report

Justice Beyond The Hague: Supporting the Prosecution of International Crimes in National Courts
David A. Kaye; CSR No. 61, June 2011

The Drug War in Mexico: Confronting a Shared Threat
David A. Shirk; CSR No. 60, March 2011
A Center for Preventive Action Report

UN Security Council Enlargement and U.S. Interests
Kara C. McDonald and Stewart M. Patrick; CSR No. 59, December 2010
An International Institutions and Global Governance Program Report

Congress and National Security
Kay King; CSR No. 58, November 2010

Toward Deeper Reductions in U.S. and Russian Nuclear Weapons
Micah Zenko; CSR No. 57, November 2010
A Center for Preventive Action Report

Internet Governance in an Age of Cyber Insecurity
Robert K. Knake; CSR No. 56, September 2010
An International Institutions and Global Governance Program Report

*From Rome to Kampala: The U.S. Approach to the 2010 International Criminal Court
Review Conference*
Vijay Padmanabhan; CSR No. 55, April 2010

Strengthening the Nuclear Nonproliferation Regime
Paul Lettow; CSR No. 54, April 2010
An International Institutions and Global Governance Program Report

The Russian Economic Crisis
Jeffrey Mankoff; CSR No. 53, April 2010

Somalia: A New Approach
Bronwyn E. Bruton; CSR No. 52, March 2010
A Center for Preventive Action Report

The Future of NATO
James M. Goldgeier; CSR No. 51, February 2010
An International Institutions and Global Governance Program Report

The United States in the New Asia
Evan A. Feigenbaum and Robert A. Manning; CSR No. 50, November 2009
An International Institutions and Global Governance Program Report

Intervention to Stop Genocide and Mass Atrocities: International Norms and U.S. Policy
Matthew C. Waxman; CSR No. 49, October 2009
An International Institutions and Global Governance Program Report

Enhancing U.S. Preventive Action
Paul B. Stares and Micah Zenko; CSR No. 48, October 2009
A Center for Preventive Action Report

The Canadian Oil Sands: Energy Security vs. Climate Change
Michael A. Levi; CSR No. 47, May 2009
A Maurice R. Greenberg Center for Geoeconomic Studies Report

The National Interest and the Law of the Sea
Scott G. Borgerson; CSR No. 46, May 2009

Lessons of the Financial Crisis
Benn Steil; CSR No. 45, March 2009
A Maurice R. Greenberg Center for Geoeconomic Studies Report

Global Imbalances and the Financial Crisis
Steven Dunaway; CSR No. 44, March 2009
A Maurice R. Greenberg Center for Geoeconomic Studies Report

Eurasian Energy Security
Jeffrey Mankoff; CSR No. 43, February 2009

Preparing for Sudden Change in North Korea
Paul B. Stares and Joel S. Wit; CSR No. 42, January 2009
A Center for Preventive Action Report

Averting Crisis in Ukraine
Steven Pifer; CSR No. 41, January 2009
A Center for Preventive Action Report

Congo: Securing Peace, Sustaining Progress
Anthony W. Gambino; CSR No. 40, October 2008
A Center for Preventive Action Report

Deterring State Sponsorship of Nuclear Terrorism
Michael A. Levi; CSR No. 39, September 2008

China, Space Weapons, and U.S. Security
Bruce W. MacDonald; CSR No. 38, September 2008

Sovereign Wealth and Sovereign Power: The Strategic Consequences of American Indebtedness
Brad W. Setser; CSR No. 37, September 2008
A Maurice R. Greenberg Center for Geoeconomic Studies Report

Securing Pakistan's Tribal Belt
Daniel S. Markey; CSR No. 36, July 2008 (web-only release) and August 2008
A Center for Preventive Action Report

Avoiding Transfers to Torture
Ashley S. Deeks; CSR No. 35, June 2008

Global FDI Policy: Correcting a Protectionist Drift
David M. Marchick and Matthew J. Slaughter; CSR No. 34, June 2008
A Maurice R. Greenberg Center for Geoeconomic Studies Report

Dealing with Damascus: Seeking a Greater Return on U.S.-Syria Relations
Mona Yacoubian and Scott Lasensky; CSR No. 33, June 2008
A Center for Preventive Action Report

Climate Change and National Security: An Agenda for Action
Joshua W. Busby; CSR No. 32, November 2007
A Maurice R. Greenberg Center for Geoeconomic Studies Report

Planning for Post-Mugabe Zimbabwe
Michelle D. Gavin; CSR No. 31, October 2007
A Center for Preventive Action Report

The Case for Wage Insurance
Robert J. LaLonde; CSR No. 30, September 2007
A Maurice R. Greenberg Center for Geoeconomic Studies Report

Reform of the International Monetary Fund
Peter B. Kenen; CSR No. 29, May 2007
A Maurice R. Greenberg Center for Geoeconomic Studies Report

Nuclear Energy: Balancing Benefits and Risks
Charles D. Ferguson; CSR No. 28, April 2007

Nigeria: Elections and Continuing Challenges
Robert I. Rotberg; CSR No. 27, April 2007
A Center for Preventive Action Report

The Economic Logic of Illegal Immigration
Gordon H. Hanson; CSR No. 26, April 2007
A Maurice R. Greenberg Center for Geoeconomic Studies Report

The United States and the WTO Dispute Settlement System
Robert Z. Lawrence; CSR No. 25, March 2007
A Maurice R. Greenberg Center for Geoeconomic Studies Report

Bolivia on the Brink
Eduardo A. Gamarra; CSR No. 24, February 2007
A Center for Preventive Action Report

After the Surge: The Case for U.S. Military Disengagement From Iraq
Steven N. Simon; CSR No. 23, February 2007

Darfur and Beyond: What Is Needed to Prevent Mass Atrocities
Lee Feinstein; CSR No. 22, January 2007

Avoiding Conflict in the Horn of Africa: U.S. Policy Toward Ethiopia and Eritrea
Terrence Lyons; CSR No. 21, December 2006
A Center for Preventive Action Report

Living with Hugo: U.S. Policy Toward Hugo Chávez's Venezuela
Richard Lapper; CSR No. 20, November 2006
A Center for Preventive Action Report

Reforming U.S. Patent Policy: Getting the Incentives Right
Keith E. Maskus; CSR No. 19, November 2006
A Maurice R. Greenberg Center for Geoeconomic Studies Report

Foreign Investment and National Security: Getting the Balance Right
Alan P. Larson and David M. Marchick; CSR No. 18, July 2006
A Maurice R. Greenberg Center for Geoeconomic Studies Report

Challenges for a Postelection Mexico: Issues for U.S. Policy
Pamela K. Starr; CSR No. 17, June 2006 (web-only release) and November 2006

U.S.-India Nuclear Cooperation: A Strategy for Moving Forward
Michael A. Levi and Charles D. Ferguson; CSR No. 16, June 2006

Generating Momentum for a New Era in U.S.-Turkey Relations
Steven A. Cook and Elizabeth Sherwood-Randall; CSR No. 15, June 2006

Peace in Papua: Widening a Window of Opportunity
Blair A. King; CSR No. 14, March 2006
A Center for Preventive Action Report

Neglected Defense: Mobilizing the Private Sector to Support Homeland Security
Stephen E. Flynn and Daniel B. Prieto; CSR No. 13, March 2006

Afghanistan's Uncertain Transition From Turmoil to Normalcy
Barnett R. Rubin; CSR No. 12, March 2006
A Center for Preventive Action Report

Preventing Catastrophic Nuclear Terrorism
Charles D. Ferguson; CSR No. 11, March 2006

Getting Serious About the Twin Deficits
Menzie D. Chinn; CSR No. 10, September 2005
A Maurice R. Greenberg Center for Geoeconomic Studies Report

Both Sides of the Aisle: A Call for Bipartisan Foreign Policy
Nancy E. Roman; CSR No. 9, September 2005

Forgotten Intervention? What the United States Needs to Do in the Western Balkans
Amelia Branczik and William L. Nash; CSR No. 8, June 2005
A Center for Preventive Action Report

A New Beginning: Strategies for a More Fruitful Dialogue with the Muslim World
Craig Charney and Nicole Yakatan; CSR No. 7, May 2005

Power-Sharing in Iraq
David L. Phillips; CSR No. 6, April 2005
A Center for Preventive Action Report

Giving Meaning to "Never Again": Seeking an Effective Response to the Crisis in Darfur and Beyond
Cheryl O. Igiri and Princeton N. Lyman; CSR No. 5, September 2004

Freedom, Prosperity, and Security: The G8 Partnership with Africa: Sea Island 2004 and Beyond
J. Brian Atwood, Robert S. Browne, and Princeton N. Lyman; CSR No. 4, May 2004

Addressing the HIV/AIDS Pandemic: A U.S. Global AIDS Strategy for the Long Term
Daniel M. Fox and Princeton N. Lyman; CSR No. 3, May 2004
Cosponsored with the Milbank Memorial Fund

Challenges for a Post-Election Philippines
Catharin E. Dalpino; CSR No. 2, May 2004
A Center for Preventive Action Report

Stability, Security, and Sovereignty in the Republic of Georgia
David L. Phillips; CSR No. 1, January 2004
A Center for Preventive Action Report

Note: Council Special Reports are available for download from CFR's website, www.cfr.org.
For more information, email publications@cfr.org.

Made in the USA
Lexington, KY
20 January 2018